John Thompson's Modern Course for the Piano

The Fourth Grade Book
Something New Every Lesson

PROCEEDS IN ALL DIRECTIONS FROM THE
POINT OF ADVANCEMENT REACHED AT
THE END OF THE THIRD GRADE BOOK WITH
PARTICULAR EMPHASIS GIVEN TO STYLE.

WILLIS MUSIC

EXCLUSIVELY DISTRIBUTED BY

HAL•LEONARD® CORPORATION

7777 W. BLUEMOUND RD. P.O. BOX 13819 MILWAUKEE, WI 53213

CONTENTS
"Something New Every Lesson"

Page

Loeschhorn - "The Juggler", Op. 96, No 11
(Figures divided between the hands) 2

Beethoven - Andante from the 5th Symphony
(Importance of simplicity) 4

Massenet - "Aragonaise" from *Le Cid*
(Close-finger action) 7

"Petite Russian Rhapsody"
(Two Russian folk songs) 11

Heller - "Il Penseroso"
(Left hand melody playing) 14

Jensen - "Elfin Dance," Op. 33
(Distinctive waltz style) 16

Grieg - Waltz, Op.12, No. 2
(Distinctive waltz style) 18

Schytte - "At Evening"
(Nocturne) 20

Tchaikovsky - "The Skylark"
(Style) 22

Thompson - "Etude in Style" 24

Schubert - "Valse Sentimentale"
(Early Viennese waltz style) 28

Bach, J.S. - Prelude in F Major
(Phrasing and clarity) 30

"Arkansas Traveler" - Folk Tune
(Humoresque) 31

Chaminade - "Scarf Dance"
(Tempo rubato) 34

Thompson - Impromptu
(Style) 36

Hauser - "Hungarian"
(Style) 40

De Fuentes - "You"
(Habanera style) 42

Chopin - Prelude in B minor, Op. 28, No. 6
(Left-hand melody playing) 44

"Ay-ay-ay" - Creole song
(Style) 46

Page

Bach, C.P.E. - "Solfeggietto"
(Style) 48

Bertini - Etude
(Arm and wrist octaves) 50

Bohm - "Calm as the Night"
(Famous art song) 51

Ornaments
Playing Two Against Three } 54

Haydn - Menuetto from Sonata in E-flat Major
(Form and analysis) 55

Bach, J.S. - Prelude in D Major
(Polyphonic playing) 58

Thompson - Nocturne
(For left hand alone) 60

Tchaikovsky - Romeo and Juliet
(Orchestral overture) 62

Schumann - "Träumerei" (Dreaming)
(Reverie) 65

Strauss, Johann - "Artist's Life"
(Recital transcription) 66

Brahms - "Cradle Song"
(Novelty recital transcription) 72

Mozart - Rondo from Sonata in C Major
(Form and analysis) 74

Schütt - Canzonetta in D Major, Op. 28, No. 2
(Style) 77

Saint Saëns - "My Heart at Thy Sweet Voice"
(from Samson and Delilah) 81

Sonata and Sonata Form 84

Beethoven - First Movement from Sonata in F minor, Op. 2, No.1
(Sonata form) 85

Tchaikovsky - Theme from 6th Symphony *(Pathétique)*
(5/4 meter) 90

Certificate of Merit 93

© MCMXL By The Willis Music Company
Printed in the U.S.A.

PREFACE

This book, like all others in JOHN THOMPSON'S MODERN COURSE FOR THE PIANO, is designed to carry forward, both musically and pianistically, from the point of advancement reached at the end of the preceding book.

STYLE

All the material has been carefully selected and arranged to increase the student's knowledge and skill in the important matter of STYLE.

Diversified styles of composition, individual and characteristic of a variety of composers, as well as the development of the performer's *style of playing* have here received serious consideration.

VARIETY OF MATERIAL

As in the THIRD GRADE BOOK, the contents of this volume have been intentionally varied and made to cover a wide field of the choice of material. Differences in aims and taste among students are pronounced in this grade and are much more manifest than in the earlier years of study. For this reason it is assumed that free use of supplementary material will be made. In conjunction with the study of the FOURTH GRADE BOOK the thoughtful teacher will assign many examples from the Masters to the serious student.

The FOURTH GRADE BOOK is designed to provide a comprehensive textbook whereon either type of student may build solidly and with profit to musical taste. If it is used as directed, giving close attention to all footnotes, the student's interest will be maintained throughout and results are assured.

John Thompson

P.S. Certificate of Merit (Diploma) will be found on Page 93.

FOURTH GRADE BOOK OF ETUDES
(In all keys)

For further technical development in this grade, John Thompson has compiled, annotated, and edited his FOURTH GRADE BOOK OF ETUDES which provides studies in all major and minor keys with comprehensive preparatory exercises for each example.

This book contains choice etudes from Czerny, Burgmüller, Heller, Bertini, Cramer, etc. and has been specially prepared to supplement the FOURTH GRADE BOOK in the MODERN COURSE.

DIVIDING FIGURES BETWEEN THE HANDS

> The passages in the following example should be tossed from one hand to the other with the utmost smoothness and grace.
> Pay particular attention to tonal balance and strive to make the figures sound as though they were played with one hand.

The Juggler
Op. 96, No. 11

A. Loeschhorn
(1819-1905)

THE IMPORTANCE OF SIMPLICITY

It has been said that "All great things are simple". This principle has been exemplified in the music of the great masters. Whereas the immature composer is inclined to include every device in the musical lexicon in the effort to create an effect, the master selects but a simple *motif,* and by skillful handling develops a musical monument which stands for all time.

The following theme from the Beethoven Fifth Symphony demonstrates this point very forcefully. Note the utter simplicity and purity of the material used. The melody is able to stand alone and requires no elaborate accompaniment to bolster it up. The *motif* which forms the principal rhythmical structure consists of a simple dotted-eighth followed by a sixteenth, thus;

 *etc.* This figure is preserved almost throughout and is contrasted

with a triplet figure,  *etc.* which later is used as a background in the inner

and lower voices, thus;

 and  *etc.*

This same simplicity should be applied in the matter of interpretation. Not always is a "chills and fever" rendition the most effective. Strive to make the interpretation at all times simple and logical, thereby causing the emotional heights and depths, when occasion demands, to be all the more effective.

Pay particular attention to the marks of dynamics and make rather strong contrast between *forte* and *piano*. The melody line is so obvious that it needs no pointing out.

Theme from Second Movement of Beethoven's Symphony No. 5

Ludwig van Beethoven
Arranged by J. T.

5

Massenet's opera *Le Cid* was first produced November 30, 1885, in Paris. Don Roderigo, "Le Cid" (the Chief), is loved by the Infanta of Spain and also by Chimène, daughter of a Count. The Infanta realizes she cannot marry him because of her royal blood and gives him up to Chimène. As her father has insulted and defeated Cid's father and he has in turn avenged the stain on his family's honor by killing the Count, poor Cid despairs of love and happiness. The King permits him to lead the Spanish forces against the Moors. News comes that he is slain in battle and Chimène is heartbroken. She is weeping bitterly when the King enters and explains that the Cid is not dead but victorious. The ballet music is from the festive scene, Act II, and the following theme is No. 3, "the dance music from Aragon".

Aragonaise
from the opera *Le Cid*

Jules Massenet
(1842-1912)

A RHAPSODY is a composition of irregular form usually written on themes from folk songs, although the term is often used in connection with fantasies on art music, such as operatic airs, for instance. The following piece is written on two Russian folk songs — the first, in *Lyric Form*, and the second in *Dance Form*.

Petite Russian Rhapsody

Adapted by John Thompson

12
Allegro vivace

LEFT HAND MELODY PLAYING
Il Penseroso
(The Thinker)

Stephen Heller
(1813-1888)

Andantino con tenerezza
il accompagnamento leggiero

THE IMPORTANCE OF STYLE

STYLE is a term frequently used in music with various applications. It may refer to the composer's manner of writing, the character of the music itself, or to the *style of performance*.

Attack and release; balancing of tonal and rhythmical effects; grace, clarity and precision in technical matters; all make for style of performance and form a vital part of interpretation. Simply to play loud and soft, fast and slow, is not enough. The manner or *style* of performance often makes the difference between mediocrity and real artistry. In the following composition the material used is quite ordinary, but when played *in good style*, the result is a musical gem worthy of a place on any student recital program.

Elfin Dance
Op. 33

Adolph Jensen
(1837-1879)

THE WALTZ FORM

18

The WALTZ is probably the most popular and fascinating of all dance forms. Perhaps one reason for this is its variety and elasticity in the matter of treatment. We have, for instance, the slow, dreamy type of waltz; the brilliant concert waltz; waltzes with a note of tragedy, such as those of Sibelius and Tchaikovsky; and of course the Viennese Waltz which is distinct in itself with its heavily accented beats. Grieg adds yet another distinctive treatment to his waltzes. They seem to reflect an atmosphere of freshness associated with snow-clad mountains and land-locked fjords. This particular waltz is most effective when played *without pedal*, except for the "Coda" which is *sostenuto* in character.

Waltz
Op. 12, No. 2

Edvard Grieg
(1843-1907)

5958

NOCTURNE is a term used to designate a *type* of composition but refers more to *character* than to actual Form.

Nocturne means "Night Song" and thereby establishes at once the mood and style of the music. The Nocturne was developed to its highest point, perhaps, by Chopin. The following example by Schytte makes fine preparation for Chopin Nocturnes to follow later on.

Note that the melody throughout lies in the upper voice, played by the right hand. The broken figure in 16th notes, divided between the hands, preserves a feeling of motion which is important to the composition. Be sure this figure is never allowed to obscure the melody; rather, keep it well in the background.

una corda = apply Soft Pedal
tre corde = release Soft Pedal

> Give to this piece your best *style* in the manner of phrasing, and play the TRIPLET figures in a clean and sparkling manner.

The Skylark

P.I. Tchaikovsky
(1840-1893)

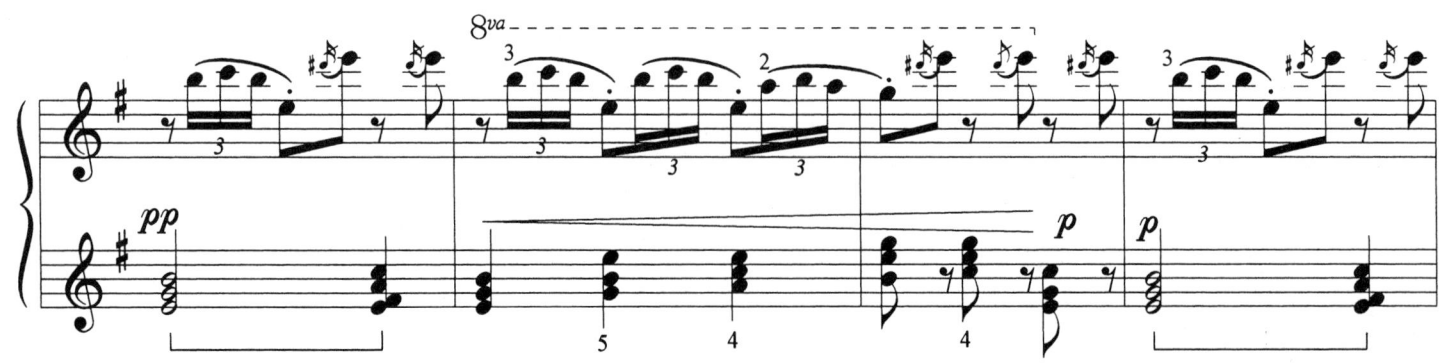

Etude in Style

John Thompson

Schubert wrote quite a few little musical gems depicting the Viennese waltz style. Liszt was so charmed with them that he was inspired to make concert transcriptions of a set of them which were published under the title *Soirée de Vienna*. The following example is one of the most popular of the set. It is presented here in its original form--as Schubert wrote it--and will prepare the student for study of the Liszt transcription at some later period.

Valse Sentimentale

Franz Schubert
(1797-1828)

CAREFUL PHRASING AND CLARITY

> Play all passages in sixteenth notes with well-articulated finger legato. Note that most phrases begin on the *weak* part of the beat.
> Try to imitate the effect of a harpsichord. Keep the tempo strict and not too fast.

Prelude

J.S. Bach
(1685-1750)

The ARKANSAS TRAVELER is a well-known American folk tune in a humorous vein. It is treated here in Variation Style and should be played in the manner of a musical joke. Follow all marks of phrasing and expression with the same care given to a more serious number and the result will be a novelty for the recital program.

Arkansas Traveler
(Humoresque)

Allegro non troppo

Arranged by J.T.

TEMPO RUBATO

Rubato literally means 'to rob'. Applied to tempo *(tempo rubato)* it indicates a 'bending' of the rhythm. Usually this is accomplished by having the longer notes steal a little time from the shorter ones. For instance, instead of playing the opening measure of the following example in strict time, the first beat (quarter note) may be held a little longer than its actual value and the following eighth notes played a bit faster to make up the difference. This must be handled with great care however, otherwise the rhythm will be marred. *Rubato*, properly applied, will add a certain elasticity to the rhythm and will prove most effective in certain types of music.
Chaminade was very fond of the *rubato* style and used it very freely in her compositions.

Scarf Dance
(Pas des Echarpes)

Cécile Chaminade
(1857-1944)

IMPROMPTU literally means something that is unprepared. The music it refers to is a composition written or played without previous preparation. However, a piece which has been written out, edited, engraved and printed, can hardly be said to lack preparation or constructive care on the part of the composer.

Improvisation, or extemporaneous playing, much in vogue in earlier days, is unfortunately becoming a lost art.

Today the term *Impromptu* is used to designate a composition which is not written in any set form and which has the character and freedom of an improvisation. Both Schubert and Chopin left us many fine examples of the Impromptu style. Naturally the title gives a direct clue to interpretation. Avoid a studied rendition of the following example therefore, and strive to make it as spontaneous as possible.

Impromptu

John Thompson

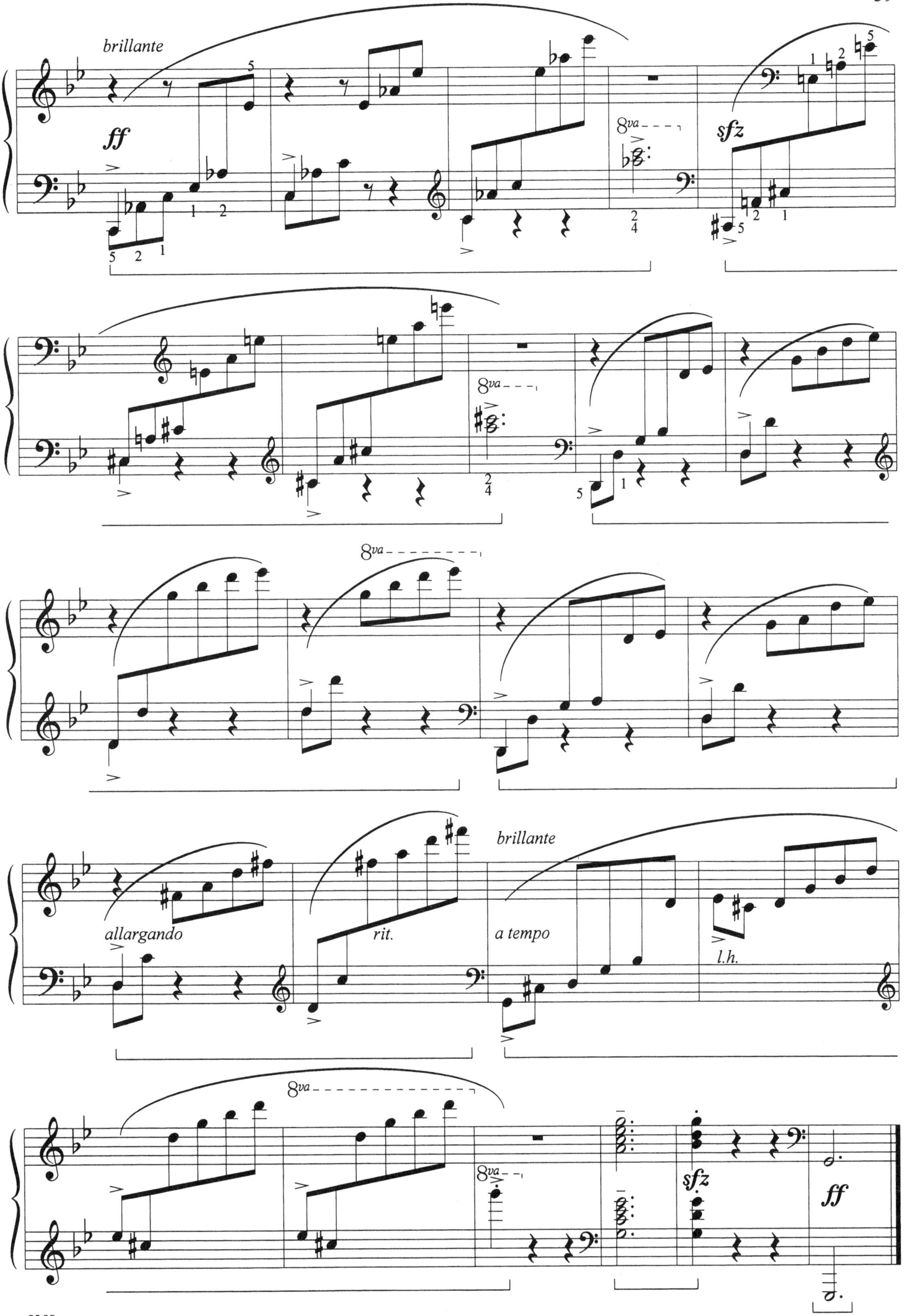
brillante
ff
8va
sfz
allargando
rit.
brillante
a tempo
l.h.
sfz
ff

MICHAEL HAUSER, a native of Hungary, is well known through his compositions and transcriptions for violin, particularly those in the Hungarian idiom. The following excerpt, adapted for piano, is from a composition originally composed for violin solo. It should be played in the style of a *Lassan* or lament, which usually forms the slow movement in the Hungarian Rhapsody form, and which was explained in the THIRD GRADE BOOK (page 70).

Try to produce the most sonorous tone possible and be sure to observe the marks of phrasing, remembering that the phrasing marks for the pianist are identical with those indicating the bowing for the violinist and, when properly performed, have pretty much the same effect.

Hungarian

Michael Hauser
(1822-1887)
Adapted for piano solo by J.T.

The following beautiful folk song from Cuba is in HABANERA form--a dance form already encountered in the FIRST GRADE BOOK.
Besides offering a charming recital number, it makes excellent rhythmical study, demanding utmost precision on the part of the performer. Be particularly careful of the triplets in measures 16 and 17.

You
(Habanera)

Eduardo Sanchez de Fuentes
(1874-1944)

While Chopin was essentially a pianist and composed almost exclusively for the piano, he had a decided fondness for the cello. This feeling is reflected in many of his compositions where the melody is obviously *cello-like* in quality and lies in that register on the piano keyboard best suited for an imitation of the cello tone. In fact, several of his piano compositions have been arranged quite successfully as cello solos.

An example of this treatment is found in the following *Prélude* where the melody lies in the left hand throughout. Give to it your best possible singing tone, follow the phrasing closely (it represents the bowing) and strive to reproduce the deep, rich and sonorous tones of a cello.

Prélude

Op. 28, No. 6

F. Chopin
(1810-1849)

CREOLE songs belong to that group which, through the melting pot of races, has set up in America an individual folklore. The French and Spanish colonists, who settled in Louisiana, used to sing their own national folk songs; but in time, after the races intermarried, their music appeared in the form of new songs for fiestas and at carnival time. The American composer, Louis Gottschalk, used Creole themes in many of his piano pieces.

Ay-ay-ay
(Creole Song)

Arranged by J.T.

Carl Philipp Emanuel Bach, born at Weimar, Germany, was the third son of the famous J.S. Bach. Although he entered law school when he was 17, he later followed the tradition of his family and became a musician of prominence. For 29 years he was in the service of the Crown Prince of Prussia, who later became Frederick II. In addition to several hundred pieces for clavier, he composed two Oratorios, several Cantatas, many trios, sonatas, concertos, etc.

According to some musical authorities, his works form a sort of bridge between the styles of Handel and J.S. Bach, and those of Haydn and Mozart who followed later.

Solfeggietto literally means "little solfeggio". The title was chosen probably because the piece is so much in the style of an Italian vocal exercise of the 18th century.

Solfeggietto

Carl Philipp Emanuel Bach
(1714-1788)

OCTAVE STUDY

Practice this etude at moderate tempo, using at first only wrist octaves. When this can be done with ease, repeat, using fore-arm octaves. Finally, as speed develops, *combine* the two attacks.

Étude

Henri Bertini
(1798-1876)

CARL BOHM, a native of Germany, was born in Berlin, September 11, 1844, and died in 1920. He wrote moderately good music, but perhaps his one masterpiece was the song, *Calm as the Night*. This particular song is worthy of Schubert or Brahms and ranks among the best in song literature. Happily, it adapts itself very successfully as a piano solo and the following version will afford a novelty for the student's recital program.

Calm as the Night
(Still wie die Nacht)

Carl Bohm
(1844-1920)
Arranged by John Thompson

ORNAMENTS

The term *grace-notes* (or *graces*) is given to auxiliary notes used as ornamentation. They were used for several reasons, one of which was to give a sustained effect to melody tones in the days when keyboard instruments lacked the sustaining qualities of the modern piano.
They existed in many forms - some quite complicated. A few of the more common ones are listed below.

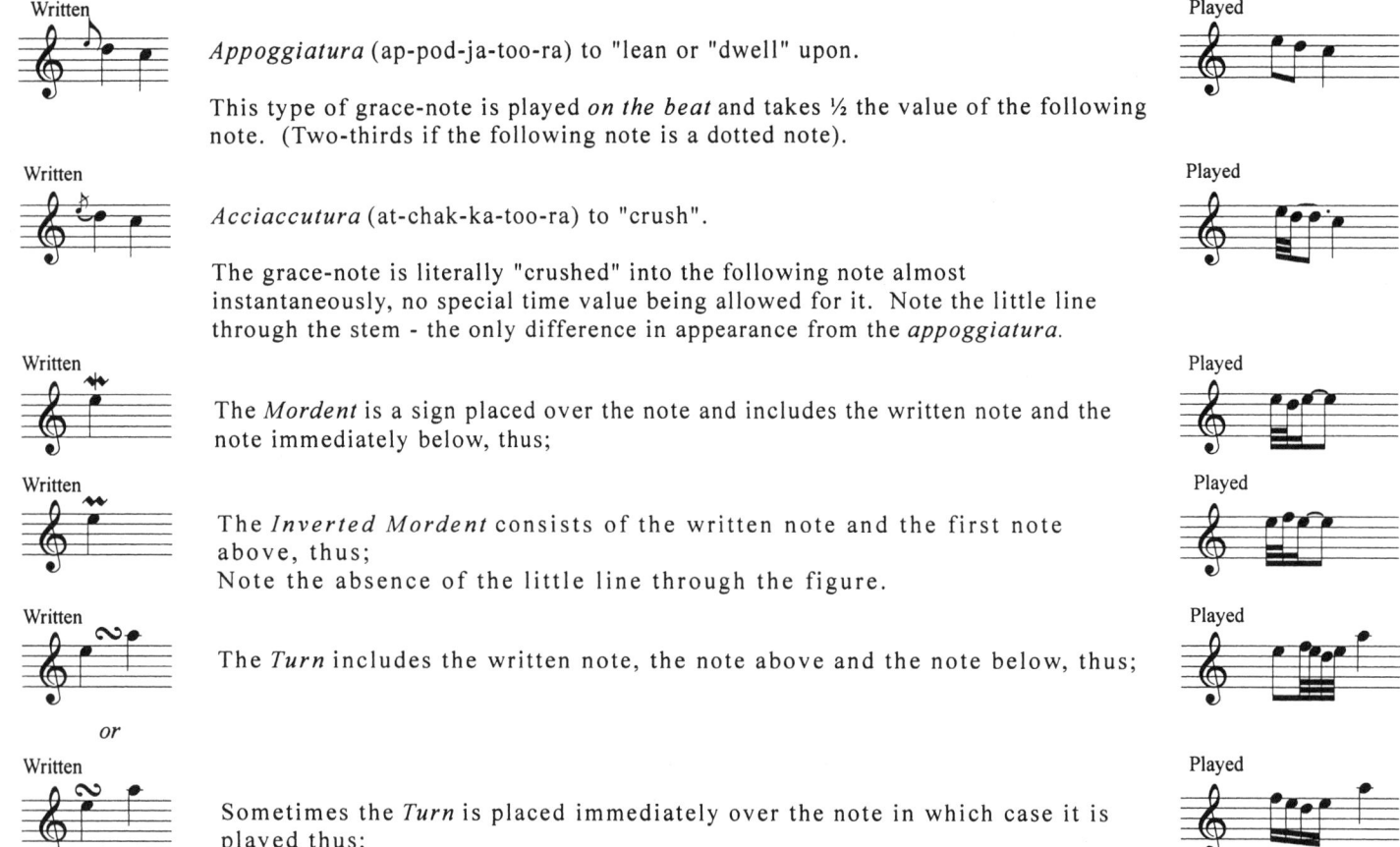

Appoggiatura (ap-pod-ja-too-ra) to "lean or "dwell" upon.

This type of grace-note is played *on the beat* and takes ½ the value of the following note. (Two-thirds if the following note is a dotted note).

Acciaccutura (at-chak-ka-too-ra) to "crush".

The grace-note is literally "crushed" into the following note almost instantaneously, no special time value being allowed for it. Note the little line through the stem - the only difference in appearance from the *appoggiatura*.

The *Mordent* is a sign placed over the note and includes the written note and the note immediately below, thus;

The *Inverted Mordent* consists of the written note and the first note above, thus;
Note the absence of the little line through the figure.

The *Turn* includes the written note, the note above and the note below, thus;

Sometimes the *Turn* is placed immediately over the note in which case it is played thus;

In modern music most ornaments and graces are written out in regular-sized notes.

PLAYING TWO AGAINST THREE

The rhythmical problem of playing two notes against three is quite simple when counted in the following manner:

Count *ONE, TWO AND THREE*. Note that both hands play together on the count of ONE.
The second count is *divided between the hands*.
On the third count one hand plays alone.

The above procedure is simply reversed when the left hand has three notes and the right hand two notes.

This Menuetto from the Haydn E-flat Sonata is written in three-part Song Form. The various themes and parts are indicated with the following abbreviations:

    M.T.   Main Theme
    I   First Part
    II   Second Part
    III   Third Part
    S.T.   Sub Theme
    R.   Return (fragment of a former theme)
    Coda   Closing section

Menuetto from Sonata in E-flat Major

Joseph Haydn
(1732-1809)

*)The time value of this grace is taken from that of the preceding eighth rest, as follows:

56

POLYPHONIC MUSIC

The terms *Polyphonic* and *Homophonic* lose most of their terror when analyzed. Both words come from the Greek and have the following meaning:

Poly = Many   *Homo* = Single   *Phonic* = Voice

It will readily be seen then that Polyphonic means *many voices*, and Homophonic means a *single voice*.

Used musically, the terms are applied as follows:
When the melody is given to *one part only*, while supplementary voices and instruments (the accompaniment) are used simply to fill up the harmony, the piece is said to be in *Homophonic style*.

However, when each voice is made to carry a melody of its own—the various parts being bound together in such manner that they form a harmonious whole, and each part being equally important—the composition is considered to be in *Polyphonic style*.

Many of the Old Masters employed the Polyphonic style of writing, particularly Bach, and one should *listen* to polyphonic music in quite a different manner than to that written in the Homophonic style. If it were possible to see the manner in which we *hear*, an attempt to draw it would look something like this:

HOMOPHONIC MUSIC

= The Melody Line, heard horizontally.

= The accompaniment heard in perpendicular manner against the melody.

POLYPHONIC MUSIC

= All parts are melody lines, therefore all are heard horizontally.

Study the following example from Bach, learning first *each voice separately*, then putting them together, listening carefully to each part and striving to make both sound of equal importance.

Prelude

J.S. Bach
(1685-1750)

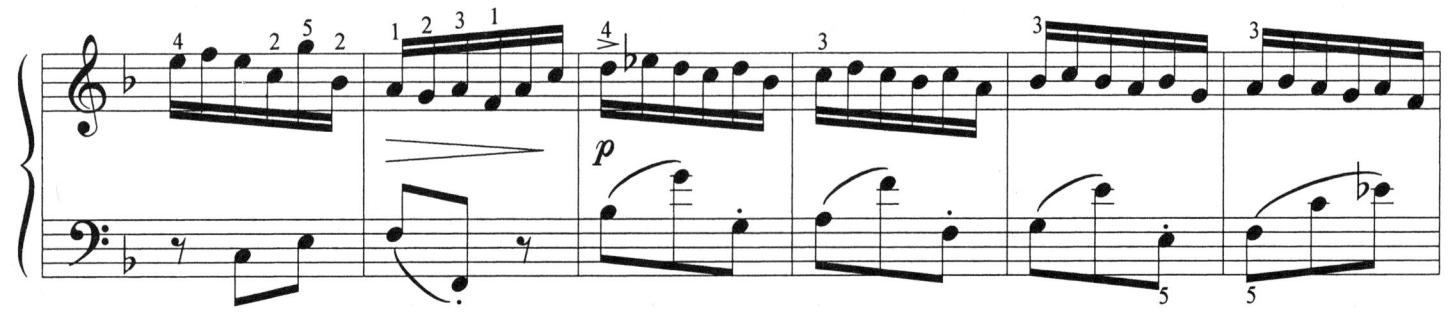

Nocturne
(For the Left Hand alone)

John Thompson

Tchaikovsky, always most effective in his orchestral works, has given a characteristic treatment to his Overture to Shakespeare's *Romeo and Juliet*. The arrangement presented here makes use of the second theme only. This air, always a favorite, has recently been "discovered" in the field of popular music and has been published in song version.
It is, perhaps, a mark of distinction when the melody of a Master can be equally successful both in classic and popular literature.

From the Overture *Romeo and Juliet*

P.I. Tchaikovsky
(1840-1893)
Arranged by J.T.

Träumerei - German for dreaming - is written in the style of a Reverie. A Reverie is a dreamy instrumental composition, having no set form, and should be played somewhat in the manner of a Nocturne.
This perfect example of Schumann's art requires a most expressive *cantabile* (singing style), and calls for clean polyphonic playing in order to bring out clearly the interweaving of the voices. Note particularly the imitation beginning at measure 7 and extending to measure 17.
The title offers a direct clue as to mood.

Träumerei
(Dreaming)

Robert Schumann
(1810-1856)

To Oscar Rasbach
Artist's Life
(Johann Strauss)

Transcribed for Piano Solo by
John Thompson

Allegro moderato

Cradle Song

Johannes Brahms
(1833-1897)
Transcribed by J.T.

The RONDO, one of the earliest and most frequently used musical forms, was developed and brought into practical shape by Philipp Emanuel Bach. It is characterized by a repetition of the Main Theme after each new theme has been heard.

Rondo
(From C Major Sonata)

W.A. Mozart
(1756-1791)

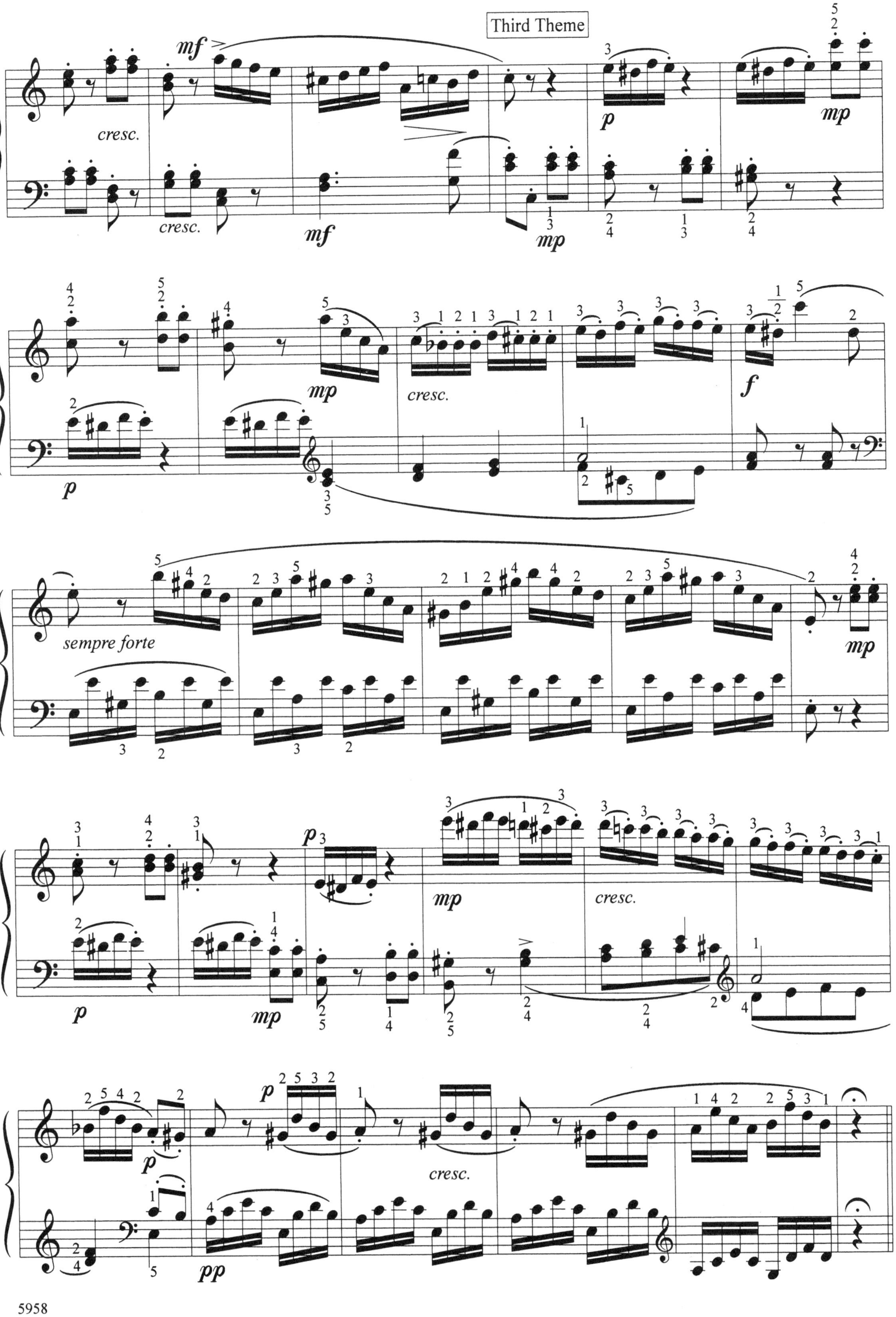
Third Theme
cresc.
cresc.
cresc.
sempre forte
cresc.
cresc.

Canzonetta
Op. 28, No. 2

Edouard Schütt
(1856–1933)

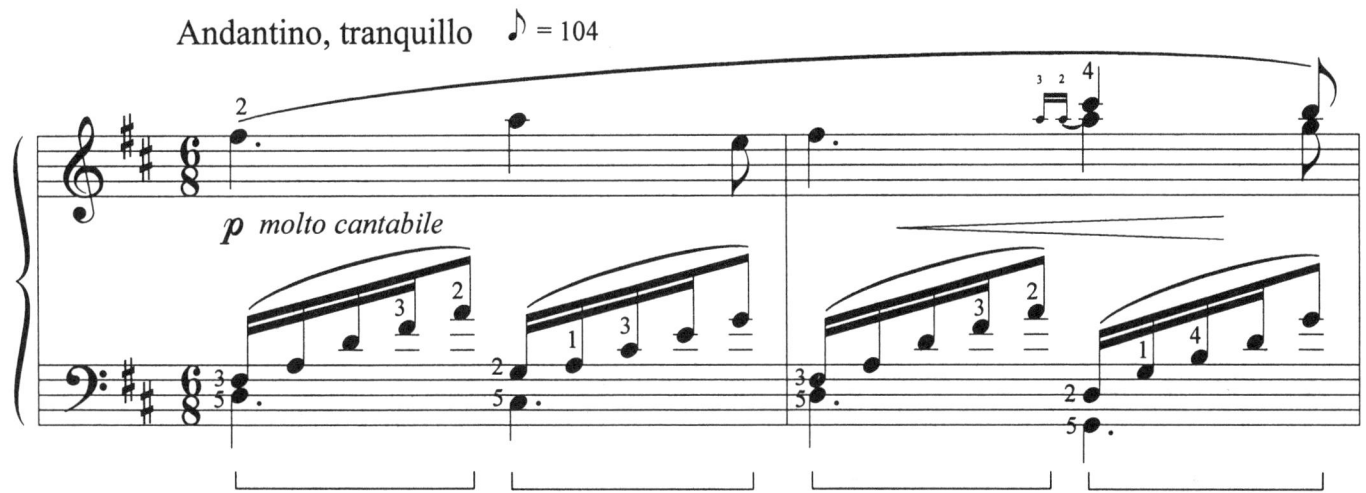
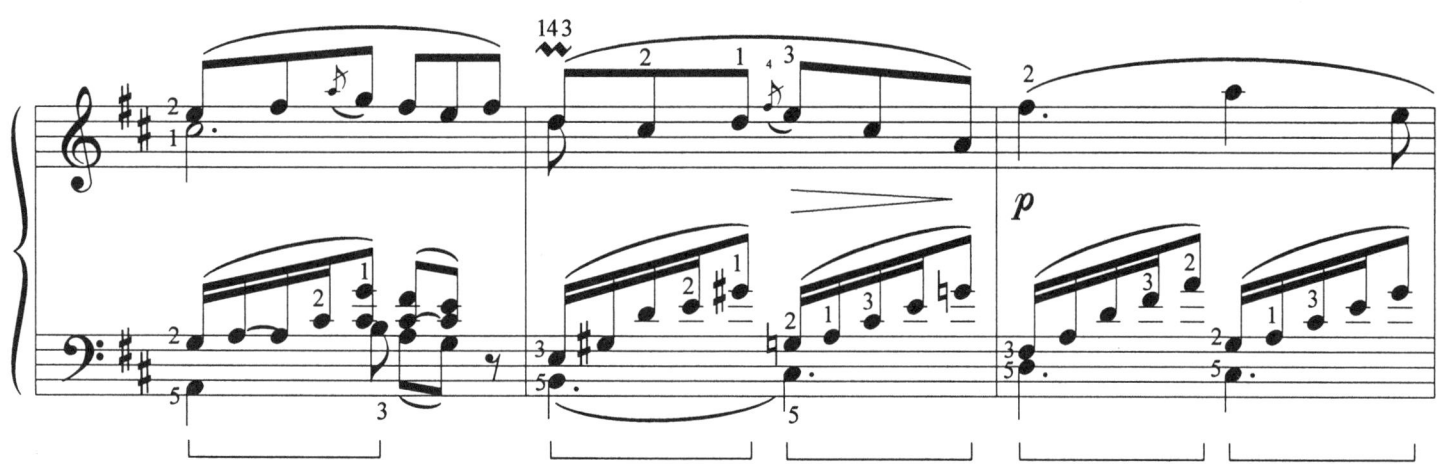
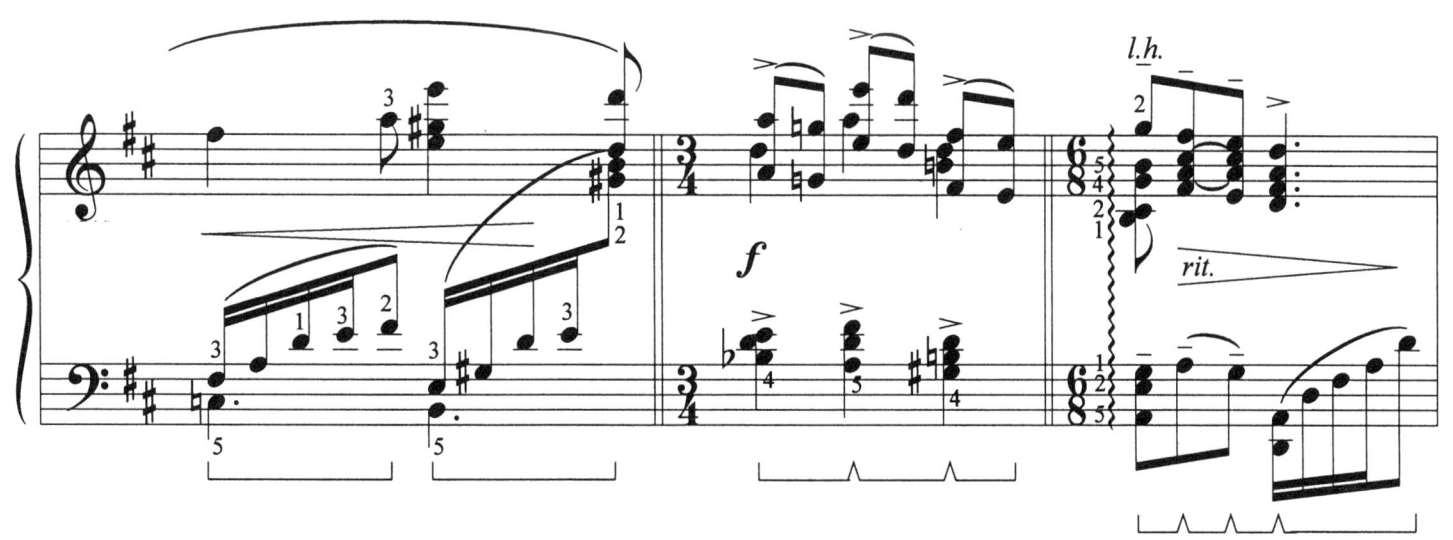

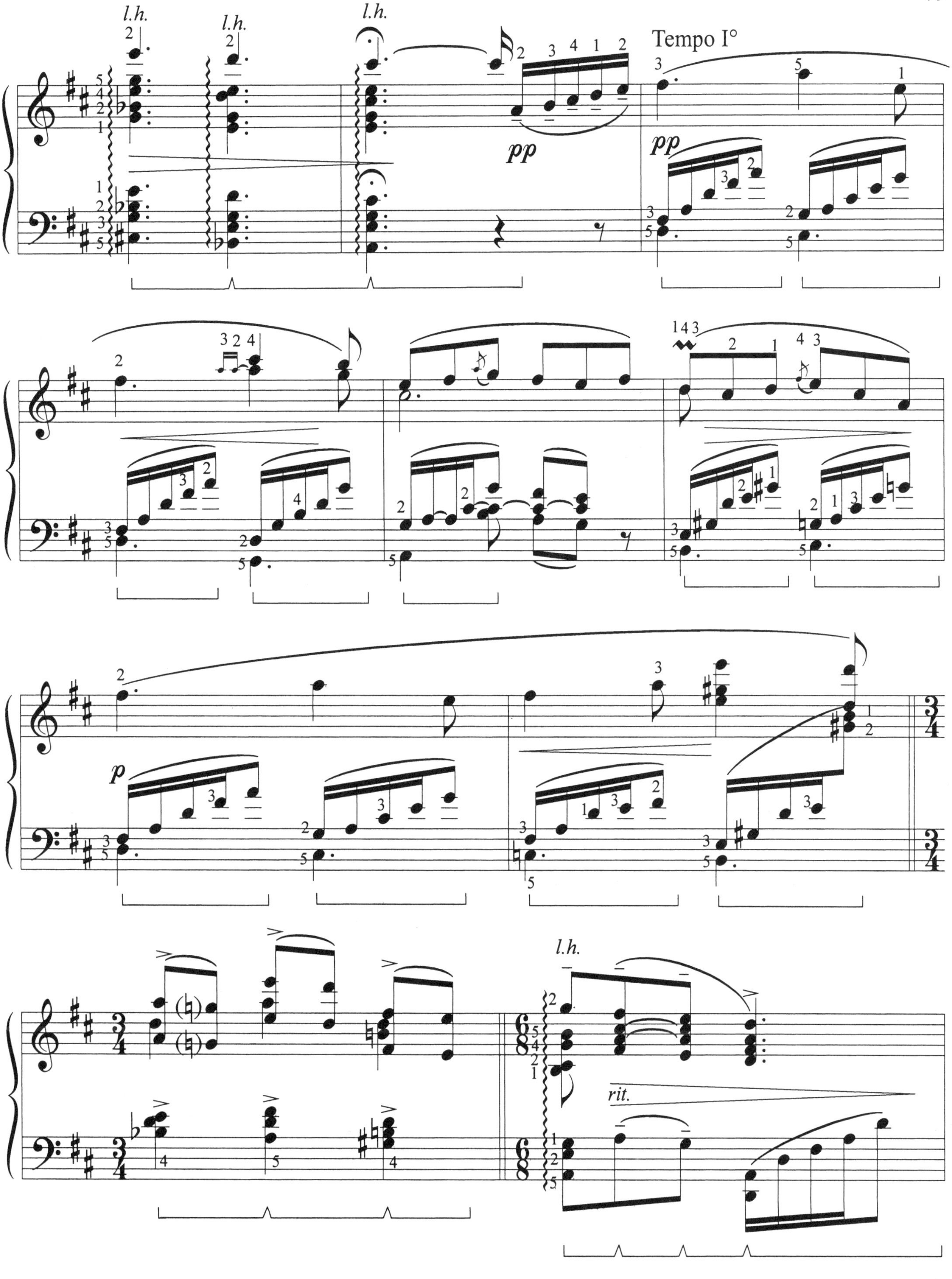
l.h.
l.h.
l.h.
Tempo I°
pp
pp
p
l.h.
rit.

My Heart at Thy Sweet Voice
Aria from *Samson and Delilah*

Camille Saint-Saëns
(1835-1922)
Arranged by J.T.

SONATA and SONATA FORM
SONATA

In the Seventeenth and Eighteenth Centuries all instrumental compositions were called *sonatas*. The first composer to use the term was Andrea Gabrieli in 1568. Literally, *sonata* means "sound piece," and the word was used as opposed to *cantata*, a piece to be sung. Later, both words took on a more definite meaning pertaining to the form of the composition. There were two types of sonatas in early music, *sonata da chiesa* (church sonata) and *sonata da camera* (chamber sonata). The first type was grave and dignified, the second somewhat lighter in character.

SONATA FORM

In order to give to music more dramatic power and more depth of expression, composers enlarged and expanded in all directions the simple forms then in use (the monotony of the older forms had reached the point where a listener hearing a piece for the first time knew exactly what was to follow after the subject matter had been presented). Mozart and Haydn did much to further the development of the Sonata Form, but it reached its present state of perfection in the works of Beethoven.

Among musicians today the Sonata Form is considered to be the highest form of musical expression. Symphonies, concertos, sonatas, string quartets and other chamber works all include a movement or movements that employ the Sonata Form. While subject to certain variations, the Sonata Form usually conforms to the following outline.

A -- The EXPOSITION
    1. Slow Introduction (optional)
    2. Main Theme in Tonic Key
    3. Transition (modulation) to some related key
    4. Second Theme in some related key
    5. Closing Theme in related key (optional)

B-- DEVELOPMENT
    1. Working out section in which fragments (patterns) from any of the themes introduced in the Exposition are treated as the skill and fancy of the composer dictates, either singly or in combination.

C -- RECAPITULATION
    1. Return of the Main Theme in Tonic Key
    2. Re-transition (working out without modulation)
    3. Second Theme in Tonic Key
    4. Closing Theme (if present in Exposition)
    5. Coda

First Movement from Sonata
Op. 2, No. 1

L. van Beethoven
(1770-1827)

86

FIVE-FOUR METER

This example from Tchaikovsky affords a very interesting study in an unusual meter--5/4.
While there are many so-called 5/4 meters in musical compositions, this is the only example of the "pure" five beats to the measure--the others being a combination of two-and-three or three-and-two.
This is an actual 5/4 "swing" with but one accent to the measure (the first beat). Try, if possible, to hear either a recording, a radio performance or, better still, an actual orchestral performance of this entire movement (for obvious reasons, this version had to be condensed). Note the manner in which Tchaikovsky orchestrates the music and try to imitate as closely as possible in the piano version.

Theme from Sixth Symphony
(Pathétique)

P.I. Tchaikovsky
(1840-1893)
Arranged by J.T.

91

Certificate of Merit

This certifies that

....

has successfully completed

"John Thompson's Fourth Grade Book"

and is eligible for promotion to

"John Thompson's Fifth Grade Book"

....
Teacher

Date........................

CLASSICAL PIANO SOLOS
Original Keyboard Pieces from Baroque to the 20th Century

John Thompson's Modern Course for the Piano
Compiled and edited by Philip Low, Sonya Schumann, and Charmaine Siagian

First Grade
22 pieces: *Bartók*: A Conversation • *Mélanie Bonis*: Miaou! Ronron! • *Burgmüller*: Arabesque • *Handel*: Passepied • *d'Indy*: Two-Finger Partita • *Köhler*: Andantino • *Müller*: Lyric Etude • *Ryba*: Little Invention • *Schytte*: Choral Etude; Springtime • *Türk*: I Feel So Sick and Faint, and more!
00119738 / $6.99

Second Grade
22 pieces: *Bartók*: The Dancing Pig Farmer • *Beethoven*: Ecossaise • *Bonis*: Madrigal • *Burgmüller*: Progress • *Gurlitt*: Etude in C • *Haydn*: Dance in G • *d'Indy*: Three-Finger Partita • *Kirnberger*: Lullaby in F • *Mozart*: Minuet in C • *Petzold*: Minuet in G • *Purcell*: Air in D Minor • *Rebikov*: Limping Witch Lurking • *Schumann*: Little Piece • *Schytte*: A Broken Heart, and more!
00119739 / $6.99

Third Grade
20 pieces: *CPE Bach*: Presto in C Minor • *Bach/Siloti*: Prelude in G • *Burgmüller*: Ballade • *Cécile Chaminade*: Pièce Romantique • *Dandrieu*: The Fifers • *Gurlitt*: Scherzo in D Minor • *Hook*: Rondo in F • *Krieger*: Fantasia in C • *Kullak*: Once Upon a Time • *MacDowell*: Alla Tarantella • *Mozart*: Rondino in D • *Rebikov*: Playing Soldiers • *Scarlatti*: Sonata in G • *Schubert*: Waltz in F Minor, and more!
00119740 / $7.99

Fourth Grade
18 pieces: *CPE Bach*: Scherzo in G • *Teresa Carreño*: Berceuse • *Chopin*: Prelude in E Minor • *Gade*: Little Girls' Dance • *Granados*: Valse Poetic No. 6 • *Grieg*: Arietta • *Handel*: Prelude in G • *Heller*: Sailor's Song • *Kuhlau*: Sonatina in C • *Kullak*: Ghost in the Fireplace • *Moszkowski*: Tarentelle • *Mozart*: Allegro in G Minor • *Rebikov*: Music Lesson • *Satie*: Gymnopedie No. 1 • *Scarlatti*: Sonata in G • *Telemann*: Fantasie in C, and more!
00119741 / $7.99

Fifth Grade
19 pieces: *Bach*: Prelude in C-sharp Major • *Beethoven*: Moonlight sonata • *Chopin*: Waltz in A-flat • *Cimarosa*: Sonata in E-flat • *Coleridge-Taylor*: They Will Not Lend Me a Child • *Debussy*: Doctor Gradus • *Grieg*: Troldtog • *Griffes*: Lake at Evening • *Lyadov*: Prelude in B Minor • *Mozart*: Fantasie in D Minor • *Rachmaninoff*: Prelude in C-sharp Minor • *Rameau*: Les niais de Sologne • *Schumann*: Farewell • *Scriabin*: Prelude in D, and more!
00119742 / $8.99

The brand-new *Classical Piano Solos* series offers carefully-leveled, original piano works from Baroque to the early 20th century, featuring the simplest classics in Grade 1 to concert-hall repertoire in Grade 5. The series aims to keep with the spirit of John Thompson's legendary *Modern Course* method by providing delightful lesson and recital material that will motivate and inspire. An assortment of pieces are featured, including familiar masterpieces by Bach, Beethoven, Mozart, Grieg, Schumann, and Bartók, as well as several lesser-known works by composers such as Melanie Bonis, Anatoly Lyadov, Enrique Granados, Vincent d'Indy, Theodor Kullak, and Samuel Coleridge-Taylor.

- The series was compiled to loosely correlate with the *Modern Course*, but can be used with any method or teaching situation.
- Grades 1-4 are presented in a logical and suggested order of study. Grade 5 is laid out chronologically.
- Features clean, easy-to-read engravings with clear but minimal editorial markings.
- View complete repertoire lists of each book along with sample music pages at **www.willispianomusic.com**.